SO-CFZ-790

So You Mean to Read the Bible!

So You Mean to Read the Bible!
Some Tips for Absolute Beginners

Gerard S. Sloyan

A Liturgical Press Book

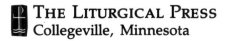

THE LITURGICAL PRESS
Collegeville, Minnesota

Cover design by Fred Petters.

Cover photo by Betts Anderson.

Copyright © 1992 by The Order of St. Benedict, Inc., Collegeville, Minnesota. All rights reserved. No part of this book may be reproduced in any form or by any means, electronic or mechanical, including photocopying, recording, taping, or any retrieval system, without the written permission of The Liturgical Press, Collegeville, Minnesota 56321. Printed in the United States of America.

1   2   3   4   5   6   7   8   9

Library of Congress Cataloging-in-Publication Data

Sloyan, Gerard Stephen, 1919–
   So you mean to read the Bible : some tips for absolute beginners /
Gerard S. Sloyan.
     p. cm.
  ISBN 0-8146-2044-2
  1. Bible—Reading. I. Title.
BS617.S545 1992
220.6′1—dc20
                                       92-492
                                         CIP

To the Parishioners of Our Lady of Sorrows Church, Mercerville, New Jersey

Contents

1

What Is the Bible and Why Read It?

The Bible is the book of the Church. Believers in Jesus Christ crucified and risen have always been a people of the Book. The first Christians never assembled for weekly worship, so far as we know, without having the Jewish Scriptures proclaimed in their hearing. Later, probably between the years A.D. 70 and 135, they produced their own writings, which—since these came from witnesses to the apostolic age—they put on a par with the inspired writings of Israel. These readings from "the prophets" and "the apostles," as they called the two kinds of selections, were read out in portions like the ones we hear today. Since few communities of believers owned whole Bibles (which the Jews preserved in scrolls, the Christians in *codices* or books), an early arrangement of readings was the liturgical book called the "lectionary." Up until the invention of printing in movable type—Johannes Gutenberg in 1456 chose the Latin Bible as his first complete book—Christians, most of whom could not read, *heard* the Bible proclaimed from one Sunday to the next. The presiding bishop and later presbyter who had done some study of Scripture explained the readings in a homily. Readings from a lectionary have pride of place in Christians' lives.

Because the Bible is not a single book but a whole library (*tà biblía* in Greek means simply "the books"), its contents have never been easy to master. The Church did two important things about its Scriptures besides proclaim them publicly on a regular basis. It worked the main points and even the phrases of Scripture into its public prayer forms ("the liturgy"), and it summarized its biblical faith in formularies called creeds. These were of two kinds: baptismal creeds like the Apostles' Creed, in three-question form as we repeat it during the Easter Vigil; and creeds framed for bishops to make sure they held Catholic or orthodox faith, like the one hammered out at the Councils of Nicea (325) and I Constantinople (380–81) that most congregations recite at Mass. Creeds are summaries of biblical faith in outline form. We might call them "safe guides to the contents of the Bible" or "the Bible as the Church has traditionally understood its own Scriptures."

The Two Testaments of Scripture

The Christian Bible's two parts, or "testaments," are alike in that the second is patterned on the first. The first collection is centered on a covenant God gave to Israel. Its main theme is the deliverance of the people from Egyptian captivity under Moses who received on Mount Sinai the exact terms of a covenant first given by God to Abraham. The main point of the second collection or testament of books is the deliverance of all humanity, not just Israel, from sin and the death it causes, by faith in the cross and resurrection of Jesus Christ. St. Paul called this renewal of the ancient compact a "new covenant" (2 Cor 3:6), quoting Jeremiah 31:31, although "renewed" would be a better translation in both cases. That term was applied to the Scriptures that described it. We Christians view the sealing of the new covenant in Christ's blood as the final renewal of the ancient covenant. Both Jews and Christians see their respective Scriptures pointing toward the consummation of all history at the end of time, when God will act as just judge through an anointed human king (in Hebrew, *mashiah*; in Greek, *christos*). He is as yet unknown, Jews say. Christians say he will be Jesus.

Because the books of the Bible come out of the ancient world, it is often hard to know the meanings of particular passages. One would need to know the Hebrew, Aramaic, and Greek languages in which they were written and the culture histories for all the centuries between Abraham (1800 B.C.?) and the writings of 2 Peter (A.D. 125?) to be entirely sure of what they are about. A further complication is that much material in the Bible was archaic even in Jesus' day. His most learned contemporaries did not understand these parts, either. No one living has all the knowledge required to understand all of the Bible. The general meanings of the biblical books are easier to grasp. They tell about the love and care that God has for Israel. This people had as its proper name for God, the LORD. It is YHVH, which as a result of Christian ignorance of Hebrew became "Jehovah" in English. Yahveh comes closer to the right pronunciation. Pious Jews to this day do not like to utter it, out of reverence. When they come to it they say "Adonai," "My LORD."

This people began to see, after they returned from exile in Babylon (587–538 B.C.), that the concern of their God extended to all peoples, non-Jews as well as Jews.

The Content of the Two Collections (Testaments)

The Hebrew writings contain books of history written in ancient mythic style. They contain law codes, political admonition (the prophets), drama (the Song of Songs, Job), fiction (Jonah, Daniel, Judith), and poetry (the Psalms, Proverbs). There is much in the Jewish Scriptures for everybody, in a good translation done by people familiar with the ancient Semitic world. These Scriptures describe the point to which Israel had journeyed up to the time of the Maccabean revolt (167–65 B.C.) and a little beyond. They are a collection of writings filled with the hope of what God would do for Israel in the future. One cannot read poetry like the second and third parts of the Book of Isaiah (chs. 40–55 and 56–66), which the Church makes much use of in Advent, without perceiving the strong sense of hope and longing.

The books of the Christian part of the Bible are those in which believers in Jesus Christ are likely to be more at home, but even they have their enigmas and challenges. 2 Peter, Jude, and Revelation (*not* a plural noun) are the hardest to fathom because much of their symbolism is taken from the imaginative Jewish literature about the last days called "apocalyptic." In fact, they are not books that prophesy the distant future. Rather, they warn about the authors' moral and political present. Again, the love of God expressed in Christ is the key to most New Testament doors. Communities in whom the Holy Spirit dwelt wrote these books. Therefore, communities nowadays in whom the Spirit dwells are best qualified to understand them. The same apostolic faith spans the centuries. This makes it possible for a twentieth-century Church to understand what a first-century Church wrote.

The four Gospels are four witnesses to Jesus' work as savior, while the various epistles contain reminders of the faith in him that people have already had preached to them.

Reasons that Have Kept Catholics from Reading the Bible

There is every reason to read the Book of the Church regularly, not just to hear it proclaimed at the liturgical assembly. Most Christians, however, do not read the Bible. One hundred years ago, one could say that Protestants read it and Catholics did not. That generalization is not true anymore. Some people in both groups do now, but the only consistent readers of the Bible are Black people of the Protestant churches and conservative evangelicals. How can that be, in a society as literate as ours, where so many call themselves Christians? Everyone knows the answer in broad outline. First, despite a widespread literacy, many people do not read much of anything. Second, the Reformation had it as a watchword that the Bible contained all one needed to know for salvation, a matter about which that age was acutely concerned. The Church had always known that, but the *sola* in "*sola Scriptura*" ("by the Bible alone") was meant to be exclusive, not inclusive as had previously been the case. Excluded were all the theological beliefs deduced in the early centuries from what was said explicitly in the Bible. Men like Calvin and Luther and their Anabaptist ("rebaptizing") predecessors did not set aside the teachings of the early councils or the Fathers. Their target was the piety and practices of the Middle Ages. Some of these were only remotely derived from the Bible, if at all.

The Reformers wished to purify the Church by biblical preaching and teaching. They believed in living Scriptures in a living Church. But because the Catholics whose company they left knew that "the Old Church" and the papacy were the Reformers' target, they reacted predictably if not very wisely. They said that no one needed to read the Bible because its contents were available in the Church's teaching. This response might have made sense in the years before printed books were available. It was not a good answer at a time when Bibles began to be available everywhere and literacy was on the rise all over Europe.

Because the Bible was being used as a weapon against the Church and not in its service, the Catholic reaction is probably understandable. Besides, two centuries after the Reformation, new generations of Protestants were teaching that if something was not explicitly mentioned in the Bible, it should not be believed or practiced. This was a novel principle in Church life. It treated the Scriptures like a stopped clock or, worse still, like a book of answers that could be consulted on any subject—animal, vegetable, or mineral. "By Scripture alone" began to have an exclusive meaning that neither Luther, Calvin, Zwingli, nor Cranmer ever meant it to have.

This spirit closed the Bible as a book of devotion to most Catholics. The specter of private interpretation began to haunt them, but in a cruel paradox it has haunted Protestants even more than Catholics. It was never thought, back in A.D. 1500, that the interpretation of one verse of Scripture could create a new Christian denomination. But that is what began to happen. By now, there are some three thousand Christian bodies in existence. All resort to the Bible as their founding charter.

It was not the Bible that caused this situation but the principle that this vast and rich library meant whatever people said the Holy Spirit told them—or they themselves concluded—it ought to mean. Catholics, the Orthodox, and many Protestants start their Bible reading with a different principle. They are therefore not threatened by this novel approach to the Bible. The oldest principle is this: the overall meaning of the Bible is the one disclosed by the ancient Creeds and councils, the Fathers, the Doctors and the theologians. The bishops of the Church in any generation and, in the West, the pope publicly maintain the same meaning. In brief, the Bible is a book that teaches the ancient apostolic faith.

Because Catholics have this principle, they should be the least threatened of all by the Bible as it discloses its riches to them. They have shied away from private reading of the Bible quite needlessly. Remember, though, that it was and still is being proposed by self-styled ''Bible Christians'' that these books would make Catholics depart from the unity of Christian faith, not affirm it. Because they did not wish to run the risk, Catholics let themselves be taken in by this false claim.

Nothing in the Bible can threaten Catholic faith. Everything found there sustains it. To read it is to become acquainted with our faith in it sources. The chief source of our faith is the religion of Israel which Jesus reaffirmed. Christian commitment is incomprehensible apart from Israelite faith. Jesus makes no sense divorced from the Law, the Prophets, and the Writings. In a word, Christianity cannot be understood apart from its Jewish roots.

Things Many of Us Had Not Known Were There

New Bible readers are, at the same time, in for many surprises. No one perhaps has told them of the cultural strangeness of many things they will encounter in the Bible. The destruction of the Canaanite villages and all their inhabitants commanded by the LORD in Joshua, chapters 8, 10, and 11, comes as a jolt. Even the phrase ''the LORD said to Moses'' may do the same. Readers may not be prepared for the slow development of our modern ethical sense over the long period of Israel's history. When did polygamy die out and why? Why could a woman not have several husbands? How did Israel live at ease with the idea that other peoples had their gods just as it had its? Many Christians will not be prepared for the religion of tender love and mercy that they find Israel to be in its later stages. They had accepted a caricature of it as a religion of rigorous justice and conformity to commands, even a religion of fear. They find it hard to be rid of these stereotypes.

In the Christian Scriptures, many sayings and doings of Jesus are reported differently in different contexts. This often changes their meaning and raises the question of what he actually said and did. That matter cannot be resolved, as the four versions of his words over the bread and wine at the Last Supper show (Mark, Matthew, Luke, and 1 Corinthians). All four wordings of his title on the cross are different. How were the churches St. Paul founded governed—by one bishop for each city or by a group of elders? Did the wealthy woman in whose house the community met lead the worship in Paul's absence? Familiarity with the twenty-seven New Testament books discloses that no modern Christian Church does everything that is written there. That is because contradictory patterns are proposed. Only the Mormons ''baptize the living on behalf of the dead'' (1 Cor 15:29), and they are a new religion rather than a Christian communion. How can women be praying and prophesying in the assembly (1 Cor 11:5) and in the same Epistle be instructed not to speak (14:34-35)? In that second passage, the prohibition does not quite fit the context. See 1 Timothy 2:11-12, written by a later claimant to St. Paul's authority, for a clue. It may have been inserted into 1 Corinthians by another hand.

We repeat, no Christians, including Catholics, do everything the Bible says. It would be impossible. The principle that holds that we are supposed to is a relatively recent one.

In the primitive Church, a living community decided what a member had to do to live by the Bible. The first and most painful decision of all was whether Gentiles had to keep the kosher laws. St. Paul and Luke in Acts gave reasons why they did not have to, but not all Christians accepted them.

Decisions about ministries and marriage, divorce and child-bearing, were worked out in the various churches (all Catholic) over many centuries.

One cannot find any mention of the bishop of Rome in the Bible or a prohibition against abortion.

Anyone who asks why is looking in the wrong book. The Bible is not an *everything* book.

A Proposal

The Bible for the Christians is a *many-things* book. In the next few chapters, we are going to be talking about the riches to be found there. They may help some people who would like to explore the Bible do so. Many have begun, on their own, several times over. They have grown discouraged. The book-mark gets stuck at an early page. People need help in a venture like this—the help of others. We are going to propose that members of the parish or a group of friends start a Bible study group. The way it works is to begin with one friend and start to recruit.

Make it couples or one member of a couple or singles. Don't let the number of people get above six or eight. Set a fixed time for meetings and do not depart from it (for example, every other Thursday morning from ten to noon or Tuesday night from 7:30 to 9:30). Start and stop promptly. Do not serve food. That way members avoid all the problems of hosting and late weekday nights. Set a time limit: September 15 to December 15, for example. Make a decision later about whether to resume in the spring.

Choose a leader at the second meeting. It may be the organizer or it may not. Choose someone with the gift of leadership, not someone who wants to give lectures.

Stay with the text of the Bible. Do not let things degenerate into a discussion of the participants' life problems (''what the Bible means to *me*''). Try to find out what it meant to Jeremiah and his people going into exile, what it meant to the members of St. Mark's community. Then and only then will the group be on firm ground discussing what it means to each one of them. Save that discussion for the last five minutes.

Pick a whole Gospel or other book of the Bible or parts within a book. Block it out for discussion at specific meetings. An alternative is to choose some or all of the lectionary readings for the upcoming Sunday.

Finish each time what the group has decided to discuss.

Use a good modern translation, preferably one with cross-references within the Bible. Discuss what the Bible says, *not* the footnotes. They may be intelligent commentary, but they are not the Word of God.

Some resources that could prove helpful are *The Collegeville Bible Commentary*, Robert J. Karris, O.F.M., general ed. for the New Testament (eleven booklets). The Liturgical Press: Collegeville, MN, 1984–86; Diane Bergant, general ed. for the Old Testament (twenty-five booklets), *idem*, 1985–87; Gerard S. Sloyan, *A Commentary on the New Lectionary*. New York: Paulist, 1975, paper; *The New Jerome Biblical Commentary*, Brown, Fitzmyer, Murphy, eds. Englewood Cliffs: Prentice-Hall, 1989; *The Catholic Study Bible*, Donald Senior, general ed. New York: Oxford University Press, 1990. This is perhaps the most useful of those cited. Do not study a commentary, however. Some are better than others, but none is to be confused with the Bible.

Many readers may wish to do Bible reading and study on their own without reference to a group, or may be unable to join one. For them and for all who are interested, the topics of the remaining five chapters are: 2. The Bible That Jesus and the Apostles Knew; 3. What ''The Law of Moses and the Prophets and the Psalms'' (Luke 24:44) Meant to the People Who Compiled Them; 4. How to Read the Gospels; 5. A Key to the Letters of St. Paul and the Disciples Who Came after Him; 6. A Few of the Tips Promised in the Subtitle.

2

The Bible That Jesus and the Apostles Knew

When Jesus learned to read the Bible from local teachers in the Nazareth synagogue—Hebrew was already a largely dead language; he spoke a living Semitic tongue, Aramaic—he undoubtedly mastered the five books of Moses. Together they are called Torah, meaning "instruction." Greek-speaking Jews called them the Pentateuch or "five scrolls." They are *Genesis, Exodus, Leviticus, Numbers,* and *Deuteronomy.* The Torah was probably assembled in its present form after the Jews returned from Babylonian exile (587-538 B.C.) Deuteronomy means a "second [recital of the] law." It repeats much of the legal material in books two, three, and four. The core of Deuteronomy—chapters 12 through 26—is usually dated to the late seventh century, coming toward the year 600 B.C. It was during the fifty years of exile that Israel became a "people of the Book" as a substitute for being able to carry on Temple sacrifice in their own land.

The year 1800 B.C. is as close as we can come to dating the call of "Abram the Hebrew" (Gen 14:13) by the LORD from his native "Ur of the Chaldeans" (modern Iraq) to the land of Canaan (Israel, southern Syria and Jordan; see Gen 11:27–12:9). Abram and his wife Sarai and their kinsfolk went first to Haran (modern eastern Turkey) in a crescent-like move (11:31), then down to Egypt because of a famine in Canaan, the land of their ultimate destination (12:10). They came back up via the Negev, the desert south of Canaan, past Sodom and Gomorrah below the Dead Sea (13:1), until they settled in Hebron (13:18–18:1). The remainder of Genesis is a book of stories about the patriarchs and matriarchs in Canaan: Isaac and Rebekah, Jacob and Rachel, and Jacob's twelve sons by his two wives and two slave girls. Leah, his first wife, bore him Judah, whose line the Bible will be most interested in, and Levi, from whom Moses and Aaron sprang. The final fourteen chapters describe the rise to power of Joseph, son of Jacob and Rachel, in Egypt under the Pharaoh. They tell of the reconciliation of Joseph to his brothers who tried to kill him, and the reunion with his father through the youngest son, Benjamin, old Jacob's favorite. It is impossible to date any of these happenings. They are remembered tales in the order of saga, not modern history.

Israel's Beginnings in the Exodus. The Monarchy

The deliverance of the Hebrews from their slavery in Egypt under the leadership of Moses is best dated around 1200 B.C. This would make the forty-year wandering of the Israelites on the Sinai peninsula a matter of the 1100s. It would have helped greatly if the Bible had named the pharaoh who ejected them, because we have good dates for the pharaohs. Ramses II is the most likely, but there is no way to be sure. This means that the time of the "conquest of Canaan" described in the Book of *Joshua* cannot be known with certainty either. The settlement in the land took perhaps a hundred years and was by no means complete. The various Canaanite peoples kept right on living there. This made a checkerboard of Israelite and Canaanite towns, similar to the situation in Palestine, the "occupied territories" of modern Israel.

The period described in the Book of *Judges*, about those who tried to establish order in the land, came some time between Moses and David. The Book of *Ruth* is a colorful tale accounting for David's ancestry, which was in part Moabite through Obed, the father of his father, Jesse (Ruth 4:13-22). Jesse belonged to the tribe of Judah, one of the twelve tribes into which the sons of Jacob, who was given the name "Israel" (Gen 32:29), were organized.

Some time in the vicinity of 1050 B.C., Samuel the priest anointed Saul of the tribe of Benjamin as Israel's first ruler. This was because the people wanted a king such as the pagans had. Samuel resisted the move, but he was unsuccessful. David supplanted Saul and ruled for forty years. His military genius brought the tribes of the South (Benjamin and Judah) and those of the North (the remaining ten, called Ephraim after one of Joseph's sons) into one kingdom, but only briefly. The united kingdom did not long outlast Rehoboam, the weak son of David's son, Solomon. By 900 B.C. the two kingdoms of the South and the North had come apart. The Bible calls them Judah and Israel/Ephraim/Joseph. Its pages tell the story of the offspring of Jacob/Israel from the standpoint of the southern kingdom which was the dominant one. That is why no northern king receives any word of praise in the Bible, although some were quite distinguished. Of the kings of Judah, only Hezekiah and Josiah seem to have won the approval of the biblical authors, who wrote from a religious standpoint. There are two books each of *Samuel* and *Kings*, although both were originally one book. They were pieced together from the court chronicles of Judah in Jerusalem, David's compromise border capital. It lay deep in neither territory. The content of 1 and 2 Samuel and 1 and 2 Kings is retold from a priestly standpoint in *1* and *2 Chronicles*. The author of these two books went on to compose *Ezra* and *Nehemiah* (which again were originally one book, but not one after the other).

The northern kingdom fell to the Assyrian empire in 722 B.C. (see 2 Kgs 18:9-12), and many from Israel were deported from the capital, Samaria, to that far-off land (modern Iraq). Why the southern campaign of the general, Sennacherib, against Judah was called off is one of the mysteries of history. The early chapters of the Book of *Isaiah*, 6–14, tell of that prophet's scorn for the weak-kneed king of Judah, Achaz, who wished to form an alliance with his northern neighbor kings and with Egypt instead of resisting Assyria—something like Neville Chamberlain at Munich in 1938. The Book of *Jeremiah*, about a priestly figure born around 650 B.C., tells of Assyria's conqueror, Babylon, moving against the southern kingdom, Judah, and carrying its king, Jehoiachin—also called Jeconiah and Coniah—into exile (see Jer 22:24). This advice to the people, to go into captivity peacefully and be faithful to the covenant there, was the opposite of Isaiah's. In the event, Persia conquered Babylonia and for tactical political reasons let the people of Judah go. This move prompted the author of the second part of the book of Isaiah, written almost two hundred years after the first, to hail the pagan king, Cyrus, as God's messiah or anointed one (Isa 45:1). All the other books of the prophets, of which *Ezekiel* is the best known, were composed between the eighth and the fifth centuries before Christ as religious interpretations of the trials the two kingdoms were undergoing. Jews reckon *Malachi* the last of the prophets.

The Post-Exilic Days

The Books of *Ezra* and *Nehemiah* tell of the painful return of the exiles as vassals of Persia and their slow rebuilding of the Temple in Jerusalem. Here begins the story of Judaism proper. Led by Ezra, the priest, the Jews began to separate themselves from the surrounding culture. They observed a prohibition against intermarriage with Gentiles and, in general, became strict observants of the precepts in their law codes. There is not much light shed by the Bible on the years from 400–200 B.C. During that time, Alexander the Great (d. 322 B.C.) defeated the Persians and made the Jews a subject people in his vast Greek empire. Under a Syrian dynasty that came after him, Israel mounted a successful revolt in the years 167–65 B.C. They recaptured Jerusalem's Temple which the Greeks had profaned, dedicating it anew ("Ḥanukkah" means renewal) in a burst of lights.

The leaders in the revolt were a priestly father, Mattathiah, and his five sons, one of whom, Judah, was known as the Maccabee ("hammer"). All of this is told in the two Books of *Maccabees*. A more memorable piece of writing coming from that uprising was the Book of *Daniel*. This short work of fiction—we would call it "docudrama"—was told as if it had happened back in the time of the Persians and the Medes, to protect its author. He told the story of a brave young Jew named Daniel (Chaldean name, Belteshazzar) who had the gift of interpreting dreams for the king, like Joseph of old. The purpose of the short book was to stiffen the spines of the Jews against the Syrian Greek tyrant Antiochus IV.

The Maccabean period was begun in glory but ended in shame. Three of the sons—Judah, Jonathan, and Simon—carried on the freedom movement under Syrian rulers. Then the Greek empire set up a line of puppet Jewish kings who declared themselves high priests as well. They ruled for a century as the Hasmonean dynasty, during which time the Romans defeated the Greeks militarily (63 B.C.). Things got so bad in Palestine, as the Roman empire called the province from the word "Philistine," that the Jews petitioned their pagan overlords to remove the Jewish royal line and put them under Gentile rule. A turning point came with the emergence of a tough young desert fighter from Idumea south of Israel, by the name of Antipater. The Roman Caesar, Antony (who took the throne name, Octavian), set him up as ruler of the Jews, to whose religion he conformed. His son, Herod, was given the title "king of Judea" and ruled in cruel magnificence from 40 to 4 B.C. It was toward the end of Herod's reign, St. Matthew tells us, that Jesus was born. Augustus, a man of peace, was the reigning Caesar.

The Hebrew Genius Is for Storytelling

This brief chronicle makes it sound as if the Bible were a book of history. It is and it isn't. It is much more a book of stories.

One can enter into the Bible at any point and read it with profit, although it is helpful to know at any point if one is reading about Israel's earliest years (the patriarchs, then the judges), the monarchy (King Saul to the fall of Jerusalem in 587 B.C.), or the second-Temple period (Ezra, ca. 400 B.C., through the Hasmoneans to A.D. 70). The narrative cycles are the most interesting parts—for example, the Abraham, Isaac, and Jacob tales that make up most of Genesis. They tell of uprightness and integrity, trickery and deceit, and above all trust in a God who leads these nomads to an unknown destiny. The David collection of 1 and 2 Samuel is like a rattling good Western, complete with a complex hero. David is a natural-born winner who need not stoop to deceit but who does, an ambitious seeker of power whom everyone takes for Mr. Clean— which, in a way, he is. You will not find better probing into human motives anywhere than in the David stories. But their main point is religious, not just a portrayal of character. They are about the threat of human kingship to Israel's only king, YHVH. This is the struggle of a nation to save its soul. It comes very close to losing it, with Solomon in all his pagan glory.

The Bible is the story of a plucky little fighter, Israel ("contender with God") who "struggled with divine and human beings and prevailed" (Gen 23:29; cf. Hos 12:5). Every human passion is described in these pages, from the noblest to the basest. The Bible is a mirror held up to us. It reflects our struggles not only as individuals but as societies. All the sublimity and the folly, the fidelity and the perfidy that mark Church and state, business and government, home and extended family are to be found here. Woven into the fabric, in every thread, is an acute consciousness of Israel's God, YHVH. This is a God of justice and of mercy, an all-seeing and all-caring patriarch of a family who is a stranger to no human passion. It has been observed that the God of Israel did for Israel all that a modern mother does for her family. This God resorts at times to signs and wonders but much more often lets the course of history have its way. Human deeds have human consequences.

Israel Learns about Fidelity through Suffering

Early in the Bible, the Hebrews think they can do no wrong because their God is with them. Four hundred years of kingship tell them that a search for the splendor of their pagan neighbors can only reduce them to the level of their pagan neighbors. Successive humiliations at the hands of five empires teach them the folly of the unsophisticated formula that election by God automatically brings prosperity and peace. Rather, God's choice of them brought persecution and pain. The reality was inescapable. They responded with prayers of the innocent sufferer that have no equal, the Book of Psalms, which cry out in trustful anger, "Why? Why? Why?" There is no poetry, no prayer to match that of the Bible. It is not craven. It is perfectly trusting before the incomprehensible mystery that is God.

Any attempt to convey all that the Hebrew Bible contains will end in failure. There is too much there. That could discourage Bible reading, which would be regrettable. People need to feel confident as they approach it.

Is there any key to unlock a number of its doors, even if many will hold fast? Yes, there is one. It is the central idea that God and Israel are forever bound together by promise and covenant. The LORD will make a great nation of them, as numerous as "the stars of the sky and the sands of the seashore" (Gen 23:17). In Abraham and in his seed—his offspring—all the nations of the earth will find blessing (v. 18). The outward sign of this covenant will be a scar in the flesh of the males, circumcision (ch. 18). Simple fidelity in worshiping the LORD was its chief condition: "I will be your God and you shall be my people." The terms of Israel's faithfulness, spelled out, were all the commands and precepts delivered through Moses on Mount Sinai. God would not, could not, depart from a pledged word that was identical with godhead itself. This people could, on the other hand, be unfaithful and many times was.

The Church thinks of itself as those Gentiles on whom the blessing promised to Abraham has been bestowed. This blessing continues irrevocably to be given to the Jewish people, as St. Paul teaches (Rom 11:29). The New Testament is the story of perfect fidelity to the ancient covenant in one person only, Jesus. The history of the Church is the matching volume to the Hebrew Scriptures in that both tell of successive failures and fresh starts of renewed fidelity to the covenant. The covenantal relation between the LORD and Israel, between the Father of Jesus Christ and the Church, runs through the Bible like a golden string.

Was There No Longing for a Messiah?

It may seem strange to some people that the covenant and not waiting for the Messiah is the key to unlocking most doors in the Hebrew Scriptures. We have to remember, though, that it was only well after the sixth-century-B.C. exile in Babylon and the loss of their kings that the Jews began to dream of a Davidic figure of the future, a perfect king-messiah who would turn all their defeats into victories. In Jesus' day, most Jews looked for a military victor of this sort. Some transformed the dream into a heavenly "son of man" who would come on the clouds of heaven in the final days. It was the Christians, searching the Scriptures once they had settled on "messiah" (Christ) as their favored designation of Jesus and thereby claiming as victor one who has suffered defeat, who read on every page foretellings of "a prophet like Moses," one who would "sit at the LORD's right hand" whom David would call "*my* Lord," and of "the kings of the earth who would rise up against the LORD and against his anointed." There is a little expectation of a future "messiah" in the Bible but not much. It was in the period after most of the Hebrew Bible was written that these hopes rose to a fever pitch. The Gospels provide ample witness to the desire for deliverance by an anointed king.

The Number of Biblical Books

About fifty years after Jesus' resurrection the rabbis composed an official list ("canon") of biblical books. They reckoned them as twenty-two, the number of letters in the Hebrew alphabet. To do that you have to consider the Pentateuch, the twelve minor prophets, and other two-book scrolls as one book each. They are the same thirty-nine books you find in Protestant Bibles, for the sixteenth-century Reformers followed the rabbis in their decision. The Greek-speaking churches that ultimately named the present twenty-seven books as the New Testament canon used a translation from Hebrew to Greek done by Jews because so few Greeks knew the Hebrew language. That Septuagint version of the Old Testament from Alexandria (LXX was the biblical number of the Gentile peoples) had more books in it than the rabbis opted for. The Council of Trent, challenged on the point, stayed with that tradition. Hence the presence of the "deuterocanonical" books in Catholic Bibles: Judith, Baruch, Ben Sira, Wisdom, and 1 and 2 Maccabees, plus fragments of Daniel and Esther.

The Bible is the oldest form of Christian prayer, and gripping reading besides. We have a few important study leads now. We need to get back to the Bible, our richest Catholic heritage. But let us not read it as a history book. It is a book of stories—religious stories—into which is incorporated a law code.

3

What "The Law of Moses and the Prophets and the Psalms" (Luke 24:44) Meant to Their Compilers

The quotation above comes from Jesus in Luke's gospel explaining the Scriptures to the Eleven as he shared cooked fish with them in Jerusalem before his ascension. It is a description of the Bible in its three major parts. If we set ourselves to say something about all three parts it will be no easy task, because the Hebrew Scriptures have been given so many interpretations over the centuries. The New Testament is the Christian meaning assigned to these Scriptures.

For a Church built on a continuing, living tradition as ours is, the New Testament is the beginning, not the end of the process of interpretation. In the Christian interpretation of the Bible over the centuries, the Scriptures were searched to yield their Jesus Christ meaning. Then, over the last two hundred years, the attempt began to be made to determine what the Hebrew Scriptures meant to the people who wrote them. This seemed to be the best starting point to determine what the Bible can mean to us. That exploration continues, with the First Testament on its own terms seen as the best way to understand the meaning of the Second.

The Bible's Meaning for Those Who Wrote It

The story of Israel proper begins with the book of Exodus. *Genesis,* as we have said, is largely concerned with the stories of the patriarchs from Abraham's call in Ur to Joseph's death in Egypt. These narratives (chs. 12–50) are more saga than history. They prove to be related to other, similar tales from the ancient Middle East. The biblical authors prefixed their accounts of these earliest Hebrews with stories that had been told in that part of the world for centuries (chs. 4–11). There is the story of the first murderer, Cain; the first shepherd, Abel; the first metalworker, Tubalcain; and the first musician, Jubal. One reads there, too, of the early human pride that resulted in the confusion of different languages and of a great flood that "continued upon the earth for forty days" (7:17). A story quite like the Noah story occurs in the older Gilgamesh epic, sometimes called "the Babylonian Genesis." These tales are all given a YHVH or LORD significance in the Bible, changing their meaning entirely. The high point of the flood story, for example, is the pledge God makes to all mortal creatures that he will not work this kind of destruction again. A rainbow is the sign of this universal covenant. The Jews could not imagine a world preceding their own that had no covenant like theirs.

This makes of the first three chapters of Genesis a sort of prehistory. They weave together two strands: a fairly late, well-crafted poem about the formation of the heavens and the earth from "a formless wasteland and . . . abyss" (Gen 1:2) and a more primitive but probing tale about the first human pair. The first of these narratives (1:1–2:4*a*) shows that God formed the universe with effortless ease, not by some cosmic struggle in which earth and sky and sea come apart after a mighty wrestling match in space; and it provides a good reason for keeping the Sabbath: If God had to rest after a week's labor, why should not we?

The second of the two tales (2:4*b*–3:24) shows signs of earlier authorship. It is a hymn to monogamy ("the two became one flesh," 2:24), likewise a primitive explanation of man's need to work, woman's labor in childbirth, and the enmity between snakes and humans (3:14-19). All these hardships sprang from disobedience to the LORD's command (2:16-17). Intertwined with the story of the tree whose fruit helps distinguish good from evil (3:1-6) is another story about discovering the mystery of sex (2:15; 3:7). The Genesis author uses both of them to teach the necessity of doing God's will if there is to be any happiness. These stories explain the origins of certain classic human defeats as well as achievements. It would be impossible to write a better set of narratives to express the most profound joys and sorrows of our race. A sorry day dawned for the non-Semitic world when it failed to recognize the Oriental gift for storytelling and began to think it had a book of history in these early chapters. It has, rather, a cluster of deep probings into the human condition and the human spirit. These early tales of Genesis 1–11 are priceless and will never die. The only thing that can kill them—and it is doing it for millions of readers who misread the Church's Scriptures in a fundamentalist way—is to take them as a literal account of the dawn of human life.

The Centrality of the Exodus

If, as we said, the Book of Genesis ("Beginnings") is basically preliminary to the Book of Exodus ("Departure"), what makes *Exodus* so important? It is the story of the origins of Israel as a people receiving the clear terms of a covenant that bonded them together. As Exodus opens, this alien people is growing "numerous and powerful . . . more so than we ourselves" (Exod 1:9), according to a pharaoh "who knew not Joseph" (v. 8). The birth of Moses is described in chapter 2 as if he would one day become a person of great importance. Christians need to read these opening chapters carefully because Matthew's account of the slaughter of the innocents is patterned on them.

Moses has an Egyptian name. He has so departed from the customs of his ancestors that his son Gershom is not circumcised. It has to be done if they are to return to their old land of Canaan (4:24-26; cf. Gen 17:10-14). The Lord has heard the cry of this his oppressed people and chooses Moses to deliver them. At "Horeb, the mountain of God" (Exod 3:1), Moses sees a bush that is burning but not consumed. There, God shares with Moses his proper name YHVH (It sounds remotely like "I am" in Hebrew, and that is given as its derivation. See 3:14-15). The reader need not be disturbed that everyone in the cycle of the patriarchs from Abraham onward seems to know that name already. The Bible is a compilation edited over centuries, and its final editors left many contradictory details intact.

The story of that deliverance is memorable. In Psalm 68, verse 9, a very old piece of poetry, the God of Israel is called "the one of Sinai." The LORD is described there as marching through the desert at the head of his people. So the connection of Israel's God with this forbidding wasteland, the Sinai peninsula, may predate the story of the giving of Torah. As Exodus speaks of the transmission of the Law to Moses, at first a hurricane seems to be described (19:16), then a volcano (v. 18). It is a powerful word-picture conveying an awe-inspiring barrier between God and Israel which cannot be broken, yet which Moses is called on to transcend. He is both summoned and repelled by a mystery that is fearsome yet fascinating. "If you hearken to my voice and keep my covenant, you shall be my special possession, dearer to me than any other people, though all the earth is mine" (v. 5). The Israelites are told they may not touch even the base of the mountain (v. 12), but Moses is told to come up to its top (v. 20).

There he receives a complete law code that begins with the familiar Ten Commandments (20:2-17). There follow laws about correct worship, slavery, indemnity, extortion, and money-lending. These go on for chapter after chapter, a complete civil, criminal, and liturgical code. The book of the covenant is read out by Moses, the people say they will keep its terms, and he ratifies it by sprinkling the blood of many bulls on them. An ark is described in detail; it is a traveling sanctuary in the midst of the people accompanied by an altar for sacrifice. These stipulations or directives continue from Exodus, chapter 20, throughout the Book of *Leviticus*. With *Numbers*, the story of the forty-year journey through the Sinai resumes. In *Deuteronomy*, Moses is the speaker in chapters 5–30, which recast much of the earlier legal material. The book ends on a glorious note: "I have set before you life and death, the blessing and the curse. Choose life, then, that you and your descendants may live, by loving the LORD your God, heeding his voice and holding fast to him" (Deut 30:14-20).

The Law

A few important things should be noted about the content of the five Mosaic books. There is no distinction made between ethical precepts like the Ten Commandments and ritual precepts like those governing clean and unclean foods. All must be kept equally. Much of the legislation is found almost word for word in other ancient sources like the Babylonian law code of Hammurabi. Much of it, too, was archaic by the time it was compiled, going far back into desert days. The religion of Israel was a legal religion to be sure, but that is a good thing. It is the abuse called legalism that is a bad thing. We can find that anywhere, certainly in Christianity. Read the "Book of the Law," then, at the heart of Deuteronomy (chs. 12–26) to see what a reasonable, just, and merciful guide it was to the life of an ancient people, despite its harsh penalties (e.g., 13:11).

The Prophets

What did the books of the Prophets mean to those who compiled them? Their authors were priests and nonpriests alike who feared the influence of money and power on true religion. Beginning in the eighth century, they verbally attacked the kings of both the northern and southern kingdoms (and two queens, Jezebel of Israel and Athaliah of Judah), decrying the abuses in the twofold monarchy. *Hosea,* for example, was active in the North and *Amos* in the South. The writing prophets tend to deny that they are cult prophets of a sacred shrine, those frenzied figures who danced wildly and issued oracles of the sort their royal patrons liked to hear. The writing prophets were serious men with a great poetic gift who could see that prosperity was corroding the lives of the people, starting with their kings. They responded with lyrical outbursts of condemnation that put their own lives in peril. Sometimes it is possible to know the historical context of the verbal attack, sometimes it is not. But the message is clear. Bribes and drunkenness, extortion and easy living have brought the country low. The kings have turned to the worship of Canaanite *ba'als* ("masters") who make no ethical demands whatever.

The books of the Prophets are, in a way, the most modern parts of the Hebrew collection. The abuses with which they charge the leaders sound like tomorrow's headlines. Yet, lest the modern Bible reader derive satisfaction from the fact that tyrants and high livers are "getting theirs," the lesson is always present that the lifestyles of the rich and famous would not be possible unless the general populace approved of and lusted after the same things for themselves. It is a valuable modern lesson. In some cases, we can cross-check the content of a prophetic book like *Isaiah* or *Jeremiah* with the data provided in historical books like Kings and Chronicles. At other times, as with *Nahum* and *Zephaniah,* we are given the barest clue in the first verses about the empire against whom the prophecy is directed or the Jewish king in whose time and place the prophet is operating. The writing prophets have often been described as "forth-tellers" rather than foretellers, public moralists who speak for God. Their message is as political as it is ethical because in ancient Israel the two were not distinguishable. Kings were to be judged by the way they did or did not support the worship of the true God and the traditional terms of the covenant that bound the people. The prophets often declaimed in a poetic and sometimes cryptic manner. Occasionally they acted out their message in plays and examples, not unlike the game of "Charades" (see Is 5:1-7 and Jer 9; 24; and 28). They would speak at times of a "branch" or an innocent "suffering servant" whom the LORD would raise up and make use of in the future. All such veiled references to future deliverance were taken by later Christians, starting with the writers of the New Testament, to refer to Jesus, even though there was nothing nearly so definite in the original expressions of hope. Christian interpretation held that the Spirit of God impelled the ancient prophets to write more things than they realized.

The Way of Wisdom in the Bible

If most of the shorter books of the Prophets and large portions of the longer ones can be appreciated without much historical background, the same is true of the Writings. The *Psalms* are lyrics to songs of which we no longer have the music. *Proverbs* are what they say they are, capsulized bits of wisdom that are comments on life. The Psalms provide an admirable expression of repentance for sin, praise of God, thanksgiving, and all but speechless anger. They are prayers for every mood and tense.

The teaching of old *Sirach*, whose grandson (*ben*) *Jesus* wrote it down, is stuffy and that of a male chauvinist, but often it is wryly perceptive. From the Book of *Wisdom*, attributed to Solomon, we learn that Greek-speaking Jews in Alexandria were interpreting Torah as the wisdom of God, playing it off against the idol-making folly of their pagan oppressors. This book was written within a century of the Christian era. Like *Ben Sirach*, it has a Greek flavor, in this case philosophical. The way it conceives of divine wisdom (chs. 9–10) is not unlike that of Proverbs 8:22-31. In both places, wisdom is an attribute of God other than God, an eternal companion, so to say, through whom every creative marvel is achieved. The wisdom of God is the knowledge that becomes the spoken word of God in the opening verses of John's Gospel (1:1, 14). This time, however, it is one other than God of whom all can be said that can be said of God.

What remains to be mentioned of this rich biblical literature? There is a love poem in the form of a play without evident religious reference, the *Song of Songs*, which the people so enjoyed that the rabbis interpreted it as a poem of God's love for Israel. Last but far from least, there are two books of holy cynicism which dared to call in question the easy optimism of those who said that God rewarded in this life those who kept the covenant. Sour old *Ecclesiastes* (*Qoheleth* in Hebrew) said that it is one dull day after another, with the dust of the earth at the end. But he knew the whole show was in God's hands, even though he could not tell what God was up to. The author of *Job* made his central figure a non-Jew from a distant land, so aware was he of the touchy nature of his argument. Three ''troublesome comforters,'' pious boobs all, charge him with lack of trust in God, but Job has the best of it all. Finally, the playwright makes YHVH a character in the play. The LORD manages to drown poor Job with doses of heavy irony. Answer me a few questions, says the LORD (40:7). Have you run off any thunderstorms lately, made a hippopotamus, a crocodile? What is your record on hailstorms, the constellations? Any ostriches lately, any stallions? Job gives up. The LORD holds too many cards. The play ends with Job's capitulation (42:2-6). The author tacks on a happy ending to protect himself against the pious and make them forget all the strong truths he has spoken. The mystery of life is wrapped up in the riddle of the universe which is encased in the greatest enigma of all: the God of life and death.

Getting Ready for the Plunge in Refreshing Waters

One of the Fathers of the Church said long ago that the Bible was a pool in which a little child could bathe and an elephant could drown. It is true. The Scriptures console, challenge, puzzle, nourish, and test our faith in God, sometimes all on the same page. There is no writing quite like them. The one thing they cannot do is intimidate us or threaten our commitment to God as Catholics. They are written in the spirit of that faith, if occasionally in the crude and cruel language of a far-off day. They have no time for a sentimentalism that acts as a cheap counterfeit of our faith. They are terribly serious about what it means to love.

We need to let the Scriptures speak to us more than we speak to them. They contain God's wisdom, even if at times we have to blast it out of the rock of an ancient book with dynamite. Our words are often not wise words. A dialogue with the Bible is fine, so long as we let the Spirit speak to our spirit.

4

How to Read the Gospels

The average Catholic might be offended at being told how to read the Gospels. They are, after all, "our thing." We have been hearing them proclaimed ever since we can remember. Some of us have taken formal courses in them in high school and college. But not everyone has been so lucky. And all of us can learn something new about Matthew, Mark, Luke, and John, even if we have lived a long lifetime.

For a start, we might point out that until the new lectionary of 1969, Catholics did not hear St. Mark's Gospel very often. It was not read much for fifteen hundred years in the West because people thought that Mark was the abbreviator of Matthew, who reported anything important Mark had to say. About 150 years ago, students of the Gospels began to conclude that Mark was the first evangelist to write (many think about A.D. 70, the time of the fall of Jerusalem, but some scholars would put it earlier). This priority is very likely, but it is not certain. Matthew probably did not find Mark quite suitable for his church and, writing some time after him, literally cannibalized him by employing more than 600 of his 661 verses, some ninety percent. Matthew has twenty-eight chapters, but the writer of Mark has only fifteen, stopping after eight verses of a brief sixteenth chapter. (Verses 9–20 were added later by someone else and were culled from Matthew, John, Luke, and Acts). Matthew extends Mark's story line, but he normally needs one-third fewer words to convey the same story. Matthew consistently shows a clearer, more concise and correct use of Greek than Mark.

Luke writes a two-volume work, not just a Gospel. In the Acts of the Apostles, he goes from the first Pentecost to the activity of Peter in Jerusalem and Paul in Asia Minor and Greece. He is the best literary stylist of the evangelists. Like Matthew, he too seems to have had a copy of Mark and used him copiously if not quite so faithfully. When did Luke write? Some time after Mark is all we can say and surely after Paul arrived in Rome. Luke gives no evidence of possessing Matthew's Gospel, but he and Matthew seem to have had common access to a written collection of Jesus' sayings. They quote more than fifty of them in identical or nearly identical wording. Scholars call this source Q; there are a couple of different theories why. It was fashionable until lately to question the existence of such a document because no one had ever seen it. In 1945, however, a collection of 114 sayings of Jesus with practically no narrative element was found in Egypt in a Coptic translation peppered with Greek words from the original. The best evidence before that for groups of sayings in circulation was the six collections of Jesus' sayings that Matthew either completed or came upon and incorporated into his narrative: all of chapters 5 through 7 (and some think 7 distinct from 5 and 6); 10; 13; 18; 23; and 24 through 25.

The author of John's Gospel may have been familiar with Mark but probably was not. It is more likely that John, who knew that a "gospel" went from the Baptist's preaching to Jesus' glorification, possessed some of the same sources that Mark did. Among them would have been the sequence of the feeding of the five thousand followed by Jesus' walking on the water (John 6 and Mark 6) and certain events in Jesus' trial. The fourth evangelist had many of the same traditions as the first three but invariably handled them differently.

The Kind of Writing the Gospels Are

To speak of Mark and collections of Jesus' sayings as sources for the other three Gospels means that the four are somehow interdependent. The cement that binds them is, of course, the deeds and words of Jesus. But we have no first-hand written account of that teaching and activity by any of his associates. What we have are four accounts produced in Greek outside Palestine some forty to seventy years after he died and rose.

If the Gospels are not immediate witnesses to Jesus' career, can we trust them? We can trust them completely for what they are, namely religious reflections on the unique significance of Jesus in the light of Israel's history. That is what the Gospels were for those among whom they were first circulated, and that is what they should be for us. These writings were documents of faith written by believers for their own communities. They were hailed from the start as "good tidings," which is the literal meaning of *euaggélion,* the Greek word for gospel. You can see the English word "evangel" there, in Old English *gōd-spel,* "good word." The tidings were that God had liberated, in a full and final way, Israel and all who would associate themselves with it. God did this by raising from the dead Jesus of Nazareth, the innocent victim for humanity's sins. In him, all God's promises to Israel were fulfilled. By the outpouring of the Holy Spirit on all who believed in Jesus' resurrection, the way was prepared to preach the gospel of liberation to every creature (Matt 28:18-20).

The Gospels are not four biographies of Jesus, even though they have the appearance of biography. They are basically tales of a religious hero, perhaps patterned on the Elijah or David or Daniel cycles. The form we know as "gospel" would not have occurred to Mark and the others if it were not for the popularity in the Greek-speaking Jewish and pagan worlds of lives of great people like Moses, Pythagoras the philosopher, and Alexander the Great.

The Chief Ingredients of the Gospels

We are sure from the New Testament that the apostolic preaching consisted chiefly in proving from the Scriptures why hearers should believe in Jesus as the fulfillment of all God's promises. The early proclaimers of salvation in his name assembled collections of scriptural "testimonies" such as we find in Hebrews 1:5-14, 2 Corinthians 6:16-18, and Romans 3:9-18. Luke uses this technique more often in places like Acts, chapter 2, than in his Gospel. Other ways of proclaiming Jesus in Palestine would have been by collections of miracle stories such as we find in Mark chapters 7, 5, and 8 and by parables in sequence, like the seven that occur in Matthew 13. The genius of Mark was that he took familiar clusters of sayings (for instance, 4:21-25; 7:17-23; 8:34-38), exorcism stories (like 5:1-20 and 9:14-29), and miracle and parable collections, and wove them into a continuous narrative that culminated in the passion and resurrection. Did Mark compose the first account of Jesus' last days? Or did he have access to one that he revised? There are good arguments on both sides.

Mark must be credited with the type of writing called "gospel" as we know it. His stories about Jesus and his teachings were probably already worked up for maximum impact when he came on them. He gave them new meaning by the context in which he put them. Above all, he and his sources had the Jewish Scriptures to call on freely in presenting Jesus and his message. If all the quotations from and allusions to the Bible were removed from the Gospels they would have more holes than Swiss cheese. The Scriptures form the very fabric of the Gospels into which a picture of Jesus is woven. He is Moses-like and David-like; the Psalms speak of him; in his person, all the prophets and all the sages are combined into one. This makes it hard to know exactly which were the teachings of Jesus in his day and which were the products of the tradition that grew up around him. Such is the fate of all the biblical giants starting with Abraham, the first ancestor, and Moses, the deliverer and lawgiver. Persons in the biblical world and all that came to be attributed to them are not easily separated. The life-giving words of Jesus are thus a compendium of the riches of the Bible and of much rabbinic wisdom unrecorded there. But it was he, the memorable person, who taught much that we find in the Gospels and more. Without him, no cluster of great writing like the New Testament could exist.

Each Evangelist, a Man with a Purpose

Until recently it was thought that the big question about the Gospels was their interrelation. How could we account for a saying of Jesus appearing in one context in one gospel and another context in another gospel? What might he *actually* have said before those who preceded the evangelists edited his sayings? Could a passage in John's Gospel have its origins in something in the first three gospels but be quite thoroughly recast by him (for example, John 1:41-42 and 6:67-69 as a way of expressing what we find in Mark 8:27-30 or Matthew 16:13-16)? Those are all interesting questions, but they tend to reduce the evangelists to editors. The Gospel writers were much more than that. Assuming the Holy Spirit's influence on them, as Christian faith does, we have to acknowledge them as four persons of extraordinary genius. They were creators, authors in their own right. Each of them achieved something that none of the others accomplished. Mark and John, for example, broke new ground as they departed from previous tradition. Matthew composed what has been called "a second edition of Mark." Luke is on record as wishing to do something different from the "many who compiled a narrative of the events that have come to fulfillment among us" (Luke 1:1).

The Main Purpose of Each Evangelist

What, then, was each of the four evangelists committed to doing? First, Mark presented Jesus as God's agent in the final days, a person who had lived in recent history. Vested with miraculous powers, Jesus disarmed humanity's ancient enemy, Satan. He restored order where there had been chaos, gave health and wholeness in place of disease and death. These were the Last Days of Jewish expectation anticipated. Mark's Jesus promises life in the reign of God to no one without a price. The only way to be his disciple is to suffer and die with him. Mark writes a Gentile-oriented Gospel, even if the literary framework is one of Jewish apocalyptic. It is based on Palestinian tradition. There may have been some in his community who were Jews, but if so, they were long separated from the traditions of Israel.

Matthew, on the other hand, writes as if to win his readers away from the newly emerging rabbinic movement. He presents discipleship of the rabbi Jesus as the way to achieve perfect observance of the Torah. This is a radical form of observance, not at all like fidelity to the 613 biblical precepts that would be developed within a century or two. "I tell you, unless your righteousness exceeds that of the scribes and Pharisees you shall not enter the kingdom of heaven" (5:20). This higher righteousness is a matter of discovering the Father's will and doing it. It is sometimes said that Jesus is a "new Moses" in Matthew, but this is not true. He is rather the most dependable expositor of the Law that Israel has ever known: follow him, and righteousness is assured. Matthew provides far more of Jesus' teaching than Mark. Mark is always describing Jesus as a teacher but proposes his wonder-working as if it were his chief message. The world would be poorer indeed without the Matthean collections of Jesus' sayings like the Sermon on the Mount (chs. 5–7). While he cites Scripture liberally, as Mark does, Matthew employs the added rubric ten times: "Thus did it happen that the Scripture might be fulfilled which said. . . ."

If Matthew situates Jesus more in real history than in the Marcan history that anticipates the end time, Luke is the writer among the four who most acts like a historian of that age. His two-volume work has the sweep of a chronicle that originates in Jerusalem and ends in Rome. It maintains keen interest in the Jewish people but concludes regretfully that the Church's future lies with the Gentiles. Luke is the best literary stylist of the four and the best storyteller. Whether Luke is crafting one of Jesus' parables of mercy or Paul's experience of the risen Christ (which he tells three times in Acts in a way quite unlike anything Paul reports), we know that we are in the hands of a master. Luke's Jesus is a journeyer who goes up to Jerusalem to suffer and die. He then, as risen Lord, oversees from "God's right hand" (Acts 7:55) the journeyings of his apostles which imitate his own.

John's favorite term for Jesus is "the Son." At times, he will convey the same idea through indirect phrases like "the Father," "my Father," or again "Son of man" and "Son of God." But he always uses "the Son." His Jesus does not preach the future reign of God as in the first three Gospels. Instead, he speaks of the gift of "eternal life" *now* (literally, "the life of the final eon"). Jesus does not speak in the pithy proverbs or the two-and-three-character parables that the others report. He gives lengthy, resonant discourses about him-self. No wonder the Jesus of John's Gospel is sometimes called "the first Christian believer." Jesus is just that for John: a man who acknowledges he is the Messiah (4:26), someone who was sent by One who has the right to send (7:28), who can call him-self the resurrection and the life, sheepgate, vine, bread of life, the world's light. "Before Abraham came to be, I am" (8:58). "The Father and I are one" (10:30). "I am in the Father and the Father is in me" (14:10). "The Father is greater than I" (14:28). "All that the Father has belongs to me" (16:15). "I will send the Paraclete, the Spirit of truth from the Father" (15:26). It is no wonder that those who resisted these claims in behalf of Jesus by the Johannine Church said, "You who are only a man are making yourself God" (10:33). The distinct Christolo-gies of the Four Gospels can rightly be concluded to say of Jesus that this one person is truly a man in whom God dwells as in no other. But John's is the most explicit of the four. His Christology prevailed in the fourth century when this human being, Jesus (a reality much denied in the second and third centuries), was declared to be of the same divine nature as the Father is, as well as the same human nature as we are.

A Beginning and an End

All four of the Gospels had to decide on a starting point. For Mark, it was Jesus' baptism in the Jordan at the hands of John the Baptist. Matthew and Luke both chose an earlier time, his conception in his mother's womb. John the evangelist went behind time to his existence as the Word in the bosom of the Father. All four evangelists possessed the historical remembrance that he had been condemned by Pilate on suspicion of harboring designs against the Roman state. To this was joined the recollection of the opposition of both the temple priesthood and the cowardly defection of his closest friends. On this basis and little else besides the Book of Psalms and Isaiah 53 from which they chose many details, they created four memorable narratives of Jesus' last hours. His death on the cross was history. His life as the risen One went beyond the bounds of history. It was existence of a new and different kind in the reign of God that he had spent his brief public lifetime proclaiming.

While each of the Gospels has a beginning and an ending, there is a sense in which none is complete. They can only be finished by being lived out in lives of faithful discipleship. Mark seems to have had that idea first when he concluded his narrative by saying that the two Marys and Salome, instructed by the young man at the tomb to tell the disciples and Peter that Jesus would meet them in Galilee, fled bewildered and trembling and "said nothing to anyone because they were afraid" (Mark 16:7-8). At least three endings were supplied by later writers who felt Mark's was unsatisfactory. The one that the Church included in its canon, vv. 9-20, is culled from the other three Gospels and Acts. But Mark knew what he was doing. The behavior of the women who had acted so courageously up to then was meant to be a negative example. "Go and do *otherwise*" is Mark's final message, so powerful in its inconclusiveness.

The Bible in Our Life

Have you made up your mind by this time to form a Bible study group among your friends? We suggested it strongly at the end of the first chapter, calling it "A Proposal." Perhaps it is not possible to do so, or you may have already become a regular Bible reader. But the best way to begin your Bible reading and study is in the company of others. "For where two or three are gathered together in my name, there am I in the midst of them" (Mt 18:20). If you tackled a book of the Hebrew Scriptures and found it daunting, try reading a Gospel all the way through, instead. It will not be as clear as plate glass. There are challenges to spare in even the simplest-appearing passage of the Gospels. But the towering figure of Jesus is there on every page to make us feel at home. He is warmhearted, inviting, abrasive at times, always just; stern in Matthew, enigmatic in Mark, compassionate in Luke, lordly in John. But he is always the Christ of the Church's faith in him which makes us feel at home. The Gospels are strange and unfamiliar territory in which we discover we have always lived.

5

How to Read the Epistles of St. Paul

When we hear passages from Paul's Letters proclaimed publicly on Sundays or feast days, it is usually hard to disagree with him. He is instructing members of his churches to get along harmoniously with one another or use their gifts for the common good or cleave to patterns of good conduct while fleeing evil ones. In general, hearers nod their heads affirmatively, knowing that this is "the way it's s'posed to be." A person who does not know much about Paul's correspondence except these weekly exhortations can be puzzled to learn that many feminists hold him as their fiercest enemy, that Jews tend to think of him as an apostate Jew and the inventor of Christianity, and that Protestants view him as their folk hero in restoring the shape of the ancient faith. A person not familiar with the text of Paul's Letters or the epistolary writings attributed to him might wonder what all the excitement was about.

Who was this claimant to the title "apostle" who did not know Jesus in life but only in his risen glory? How did he become so influential in the early Church and remain so ever since? Was it only on the strength of his correspondence? And how seriously do believers have to take his writings if they find themselves in disagreement with one or the other of his teachings?

St. Paul was, first of all, the earliest follower to record anything of the Jesus Christ movement that we possess. The Let-

ters that he *surely* wrote are seven in number. They were probably written over the years A.D. 50 through 57. A decade and
a half of correspondence that no one bothered to save may have
preceded what we have. Paul was a "diaspora" Jew, a word
meaning sown or scattered. It referred to those Jews living
throughout the Mediterranean world. He came from eastern
Asia Minor (modern Turkey near the Syrian border). Greek
was his native language, not Aramaic. He had a good Jewish
education and was probably a young proselytizer of the Phari-
see persuasion—their members were separatist, ritual observants—before he turned around in his tracks. We know what
we do about him from two distinct sources. There are a few
autobiographical details in his Letters (Gal 1:11–2:14; Phil 3:3–6;
1 Cor 15:1–11; 2 Cor 1:21–12:10), but the content of the Letters
themselves tells us just as much about him. Secondly, there
is the account of his travels and preaching by someone who
admired him greatly, the author of Luke-Acts. Luke may have
known him at first hand, but since he does not seem to have
known the content of Paul's Gospel very well, many scholars
assume that he worked from sources such as a travel journal.

The Epistles in Relation to Crises

The most important thing about Paul's Letters to the
churches is their occasional character. He never recorded how
he presented the Gospel for the first time to a new community or how he gained access to one. We have to deduce what
he thought were the most important aspects of the Gospel he
preached and how, if at all, it differed from the religion of Israel apart from the person of Jesus Christ. All these matters
we must conclude from the fragmentary record he left behind.
He wrote exclusively to deal with situations in his churches.
From Paul's vocabulary (i.e., an actual word-count) and style,
it has been deduced that he was certainly the author of these
seven Letters: *Romans, 1* and *2 Corinthians, Galatians, Philippians, 1 Thessalonians,* and *Philemon.* Rome, Corinth, Philippi,
and Thessalonica were cities; Galatia was a province. Phile-

mon was a wealthy Christian whose slave Onesimus had run off, met Paul, and been baptized. The reason *2 Thessalonians* does not appear in this list is that it resembles 1 Thessalonians very closely, making many scholars suspect that a second-generation disciple composed it to resolve the problems that the first Letter created.

Colossae was a city in the province the Romans called Asia and old geography books refer to as Asia Minor (modern Turkey). The Letter to its community contains themes from Paul's preaching, with one or two exceptions. But the writing style is not his, hence the suspicion that a disciple wrote it for him. *Ephesians* is a brief anthology that faithfully records Paul's major concerns. It was composed a generation after his death for churches completely Gentile in makeup. The two Epistles to Timothy and the one to Titus, the so-called "pastorals," likewise betray another hand. The authors had different interests from Paul, such as church organization, that he shows no concern for, and they held a few positions quite opposed to his. The custom of writing under another's name may surprise us. Forgery is not the proper term for it, but rather "pseudonymous authorship." In the ancient world, people circulated writings that claimed to be the work of those whose sponsorship they looked for. If St. Paul did not write this letter, the theory went, he very well might have.

Each of Paul's epistles has a specific purpose. Usually it is to settle a dispute or a problem. That is the first thing to look for as we read through a Letter. Some of them, however, give evidence of being stitched together from several different Letters. That makes a single purpose hard to identify. 2 Corinthians, for example, seems to be composed of at least four Letters and Philippians, for all its brevity, of more than one. The way to tell that this has happened is by identifying a sharp break in thought or style (a "seam"), something that "does not follow." Check out 2 Corinthians as it leads up to 2:13. Then skip to 7:5 and see if it does not logically resume there. This means that 2:14 through 7:4 were inserted at this point.

Similarly, chapters 8 and 9 seem placed side by side because they treat the same theme; 10 through 13 are a unit that can stand alone; and 6:14 through 7:1 appear to be an angry interval between the conciliatory passages that end at 6:13 and resume at 7:2. So we have what are edited versions of some of this correspondence. Remember, too, that there were no chapters or verses when Paul wrote his letters.

The Purposes of the Different Letters

Most of the Epistles, however, give evidence of having been written at one time and with one purpose. What are some of these purposes? *1 Thessalonians* is largely written in praise of the recipients' faith, but Paul wishes to set their minds at rest on one thing. They need not worry that at the Lord's Coming they will have an advantage over those family members and friends who have died before them. As part of this consolation, Paul paints a word picture of what a nineteenth-century evangelical would call "the rapture," namely, being caught up in the clouds to meet the Lord in the air (4:13-17). This was standard apocalyptic imagery. Yet the *Second Letter to the Thessalonians* exists—whether written by Paul or another—to relieve the disturbance of mind caused by this attempt at consolation in the *First Letter* (see 2 Thess 2:1-12). The two epistles provide a good lesson in the perils Paul experienced in presenting the Gospel in categories with which his Jewish compatriots were at home but which were foreign to pagan Greeks. It is a good lesson for us about our taking literally the imaginative word pictures of a distant time. That Jesus will come in glory at the end is at the heart of our faith. Exactly how or when no one knows. St. Paul was clear that the *time* was a complete mystery (1 Thess 5:1-11). It would have helped if he had made clear that he knew nothing of the *circumstances*. Paul and all the New Testament writers came out of the mold of apocalyptic Judaism. It is a world we have never inhabited and cannot begin to understand. Interpreting its imagery literally only makes us look foolish.

The *First Letter to the Corinthians* was written to censure the community for its factionalism along social and economic lines. It also answered queries about sex and marriage, and how seriously to take the pagan practice of dedicating food to the gods at the market before the butchers sold it. Some wonderful teaching about the Eucharist as the sign of unity and about the necessity for the resurrection of the dead appears in this epistle. *2 Corinthians* goes in several directions, chiefly detailing Paul's deep hurt over a rebuff by someone in this community. But he also writes about the collection he is taking up in all of his Gentile churches for the relief of the Jewish churches of Palestine. Clearly, Paul thinks the collection will have great symbolic value in bringing Jews and Gentiles together in the Church.

Philippi was the capital of Macedonia in northern Greece (nowadays it is a ruin; the nearest village is named Lydia). The community there was Paul's favorite among his churches because of its many kindnesses to him (see Phil 4:10-20). This *short letter* is therefore warm in tone, but it makes a sharp break at 3:2 with its warning against those who were forcing circumcision on Gentile believers. Someone has evidently required it of Paul's Gentiles in *Galatia*. He writes them *an angry letter*, saying they have let themselves be bewitched, literally, by a spell (Gal 3:1). There is much in that Letter about how Law observance has to follow circumcision, a fact that the Galatians do not seem to realize, and how Gentiles who formerly had to take on the yoke of the Law as Jewish proselytes to be right with God no longer have to do so. That requirement, Paul argues, was meant for Jews, and with faith in Christ's death and resurrection, Gentiles no longer need to conform to it.

After writing to Galatia, Paul addresses the *Roman* community, one that he had not evangelized, saying he hopes to visit them on the way to Spain after he has first brought the results of his collection to Judea (see Rom 15:22-29). But he is fearful that his fellow Jews there will not receive him kindly, neither the "saints" (the baptized) nor "unbelievers" (the non-Jesus Jews; see v. 31). He sets out the Gospel he has been presenting as it touches the lives, first of Gentiles, then of Jews (chs. 1–8). This is in preparation for the heart of the Letter (9–11), a reflection on what God's mysterious plan for the Jews may be. Paul knows that they have not received the Gospel in great numbers in his almost twenty-five-year ministry, and this baffles him. All he can be sure of is that the God of Israel cannot, will not, desert this covenanted people claimed as the LORD's own.

The relation of Jews to non-Jews has not been a lively question in the Church in 1,850 years. Yet we keep dealing with it as if it were a current topic. Faith in God of the quality of Abraham's—for which the proper modern term is perfect trust—will always be the basic condition of being in a good relation with God. That is a perennial demand of Christian life. But to set faith and ''works of the law''—whatever that phrase might have meant—in opposition to each other is to revive a first-century Jewish debate on Reformation terms in a way that is practically meaningless in modern times. There is, to be sure, a mechanical understanding of religion that those who practice any religion can fall into. It is essential to be on guard against it, and St. Paul is very helpful in this matter. But in dictating his Letters at high speed, he meant to deal with matters that were pressing in his day. We would be wrong to look for an answer in them to every problem of *our* day. Certainly, there is no Jewish-Gentile problem in the Church in our day remotely like anything Paul faced. There will always be, of course, the need for total reliance on God and a repudiation of anything smacking of satisfaction once we have performed religious acts (like reading the Bible).

Some Things Not to Look for, and to Look for, in Paul

There were matters St. Paul was not engaged in: (1) writing a summary of dogmas for the Church for all time to come; (2) writing a handbook of disciplinary practice for the churches of all time to abide by; (3) spelling out the relation of Gentile Christians to Jews for all time on the basis of the fact that in his relatively brief career he could not understand why his message was not widely accepted by fellow Jews. It cannot be said too strongly that, while St. Paul was testifying to apostolic practice in his place and time, he was not legislating for all generations that would follow him. He had no idea that there would *be* such a future. Paul wrote under the inspiration of the Holy Spirit. He was a representative of that apostolic age that is the foundation of Christian life. At the same time, he does not, cannot, make us prisoners of his culture or outlook. His views on slavery or the male ascendancy over women or Jewish apocalyptic writing are not our views. What we need to learn from him is how to be true in our day to the Gospel that he preached in his day.

These are some of the great teachings to look for, listed as statements, as we struggle with the priceless treasure of Paul's epistles: (1) The unity to which God has called us in Christ is no less than a being *in* Christ, members of his body at the service of one another with our variety of gifts. (2) We are in a relation with God and each other that is superior to that of humanity at the start, in virtue of the grace that has been poured out in our hearts because we believe in the risen Christ. (3) Our calling is to grow up to the full stature of Christ, leaving behind us the things of infancy and childhood, in order to become mature in the Christ who is our life. (4) We must live the kind of moral life that befits our calling, with a view always to the effects of our actions on the body, namely the body of believers. (5) We need to pray always, commending each other to Jesus the Lord and to God, remembering at the same time the needs of those who are outside the household of faith.

In reading St. Paul's epistles, we are constantly surprised by the nuggets of practical wisdom embedded in his loftiest discourses. He is an eminently *usable* genius. We are alternately attracted by his warmhearted concern for individuals and communities and repelled by his stern settlements regarding deviants from the straight path. He is by turns compassionate, sarcastic, rational, emotional, and calmly judicious. But above all, he is caring. Paul provides a remarkable example of care for other human beings, modeled on the care God first has for us. There is something in Paul for all. That is because there are several Pauls. We must choose the one who is most helpful to us from among the several in this many-sided man. It is likely to be close to the selection that the Church of the ages has made.

A Course of Bible-Reading Action

The first thing we have to do is to build in a little leisure for Bible reading. Leisure is a word for available psychological space, the time we make time for. Normally, no one devotes leisure time to anything that is not pleasurable. The Bible, once attacked on good terms, proves to be not only good for us (like medicine or duty) but good in itself, which means encounter with it can be a pleasure. It is the inspired word of God and the book of the Church, but it is also interesting, exciting, maddening, consoling, and instructive. It is above all nourishing: not thin gruel or milk for babies but meaty reading, something we can sink our teeth into. Something that can sink its teeth into us.

Toward the end of Chapter 1, we mentioned some paperback books that could be useful in resolving dilemmas about difficult passages. There, we strongly recommended forming small groups for Bible study: for a limited series of meetings (say eight successive weeks), for a limited span of time (say 7:30 to 9:30, *sharp*). The human dynamics in any such group study are extremely important. Bad leadership or no leadership can kill a group in short order. What makes a good group leader? Not necessarily learning or zeal for the project. Insight is the best qualification for leadership in a venture like this: seeing how different kinds of people (the assertive, the shy, the uninformed, the well-informed) can be helped to work together and seeing what lies *behind* the book or passage of the Bible that the group has chosen for study. A good leader comes to every session ready (if the need arises) to raise good questions. Most of these questions will be in the realm of fact: "Could Jesus possibly have said such a thing in solidly Jewish Galilee?" or "Why do the speeches of Peter and Paul in Acts sound nearly identical?" But other questions, *toward the end of the evening,* will be in the realm of reflection. "What is there about the prophet's challenge to the king that is timeless, even in times like ours?" "How can the teaching of Jesus or the Epistle of James or 1 John be transposed into a modern key?"

Bad leadership or no leadership kills good groups. When we assemble, Bibles in hand, we have dynamite, nuclear power in our midst. We must choose one of our number who can handle it with care and handle us with care.

6

A Few of the Tips Promised in the Subtitle

1. *Getting the Point.* The Bible in both its parts is a collection of ancient writings from the Semitic world. Some fragments are not merely ancient but archaic, therefore presumably not fully understood even by the persons who incorporated them. We cannot expect to comprehend it upon a simple reading or re-reading. There is enough there to nourish our religious spirit. Just remember how much eludes even the most learned persons in the study of the Bible.

2. *The Bible in English.* If the study group compares the English translations that different members possess and learns that the various renderings differ widely at times, let the students not be dismayed. The same Hebrew and Greek passages can be translated in a variety of ways, all of which will be faithful to the original languages. Sometimes the textual witnesses (i.e., the oldest and best manuscripts) differ, and translators have to make a choice, even to the point of guessing at phrases that, as they stand, do not make sense. Differences more often are caused by the set of principles by which a translating team works: e.g., a verbal equation theory where one word always stands for another or a theory of "dynamic equivalence" that answers the question "How would we say this in English since we cannot say it the way Hebrew or Greek does?" Do not crow over possessing "a really good translation." Those done after 1945 (except that unscholarly paraphrase *The Way*) all have their

virtues and are generally superior to those done before that date because of the immense advances in Bible knowledge. Every translation is a new composition and is bound to be, in some measure, a betrayal of the original.

3. *Biblical Morals.* Ancient Israel had codes of revenge and practices in war, in the possession of goods, and in marriage that are separated by a world from what Jews and Christians consider ethical today. The New Testament tells of a number of updatings of behavior among adherents to the apostolic Christian faith. The refinement has continued over the centuries. Judaism did the same in its midrashic and Talmudic writings which Christians tend not to know. They make the mistake of thinking that only in Christianity has there been this kind of moral and religious advancement. The two collections of Scripture are blueprints for two religions, a mother and a daughter. The religions at many points do not resemble their founding documents.

4. *Interpreting the Bible.* Do not take seriously the claim of Christians who say that they are faithful to every word of God in the Bible. There are no such people, nor could there be. One basic reason is that the Second Testament, that of the Christians, went in several fresh directions from the First Testament of the Jews. Christians retained the Jewish Scriptures as their religious history but not their ethnic history or their ritual practice. Almost from the start, believers in Jesus Christ interpreted these Scriptures "spiritually," as they put it, meaning that they understood the books of the collection figuratively and not literally. Christians have done the same with parts of the books in the Second Testament from the year A.D. 150 onward, when these writings began to be collected and widely known. That is because there are different understandings of Jesus there, different patterns of community (i.e., local church) organization, different understandings and practices in matters as basic as baptism and fasting. The best test for fidelity to the Scriptures is adherence to the living tradition that first accepted the Bible of the Jews, then produced its own writings, and after a considerable period began to live with all of these Scriptures

as their guide. Such adherence has been extremely various, as reading Christian writings of the third, the fifth, or the fifteenth century will disclose. "Interpret Scripture by Scripture" is a helpful principle, but it does not solve every problem. Looking to what the believers of the centuries have made of these writings does. If that sounds like depending on the Christian community for its interpretation of the Bible, that is exactly what it is. Whether a Church has 893 million members or is an independent congregation of eighty-one, it is its tradition that interprets Scripture.

5. *Learning about Interpretation.* As we read the Bible, we will often ask ourselves, "Why do we do *this* when this passage says to do *that*?" or "Why don't we do this when the Bible tells us to do it?" The answer to these questions is buried deep in Church history, which is at the same time a history of interpreting the Bible. That is a separate study from studying the text of the Bible. Do it if the group has time for it. Or invite someone to come to a meeting who knows a lot about the faith of the early Church, the Middle Ages, and the Reformation.

6. *When the Bible Quotes the Bible.* It is good to use a Bible for study that has footnotes or sidenotes referring to other places in the Bible and to look them up. We will discover a number of important things. When something is said by an evangelist other than the one we are working from, the context will differ and sometimes give the passage a different meaning. Or there may be a different angle to what St. Paul says (like marriage partners separating in certain circumstances with freedom to remarry) than to what Jesus says (about neither partner being free to get rid of the other). When we look up a biblical text quoted by a New Testament writer we will find that the earliest Church, like the Rabbis, was not in the least worried about exact quotation. When they quoted, the new context often changed the original meaning. Nowadays, we are terribly concerned about "not quoting out of context." In the ancient world, the new context provided a new meaning for the text.

7. *How Commentators Help.* If we use a Bible with footnotes, we need to remember that the footnotes are not inspired. The Bible is. Often the notes provide invaluable help (for example, when they tell us the probable meaning of the Egyptian name "Moses" and how the Hebrews played the game "sounds-like" with it: Mosheh sounds like the Hebrew *mashah*, to "draw out"). But when footnotes tell us the meaning of a verse or passage, they are the scholarly opinion of a team of writers and do not become the only opinion possible just because they are printed in a Bible. Chances are the opinion will be correct, but even when it is wrong or slightly off the mark, it can get a good discussion going—the kind that resulted in the framing of this particular footnote in the first place.

8. *Recycled Material.* Let us not be surprised to find repetition in the Bible. Whole portions of writings in the First Testament are reemployed by later authors. Checking out cross-references will yield long passages repeated almost verbatim. Remember, Matthew uses ninety percent of the verses in Mark often word for word. The author of Ephesians drew heavily on Colossians; the anonymous writer of 2 Peter relied on Jude.

9. *Who Were the Human Authors?* It is not at all certain who wrote the books of the Bible. The exceptions are the few cases where they identify themselves, as when John of Patmos says he wrote the book we know as Revelation or St. Paul signs his Letters. The Books of Ruth and Jonah, Job and Daniel are about characters by those names, written about in the stories. When the writers of the early second century quoted the Gospels, they never said, "as Matthew writes" or "as we read in John," so we assume the Gospels got their names after that. The earliest naming of the evangelists comes around A.D. 180. There must have been a reason to attach each Gospel to a person by that name (two of them were Jesus' disciples), but we do not know what it was. As with the naming of the books of the prophets, the teachings contained in the Gospels went back somehow to four remembered persons.

10. *Who Wrote What Some Claimed?* Another thing to be clear on is the practice of pseudonymous authorship. Writers at-

tached the name of an important person to a writing to gain acceptance for it, even pretending they *were* that person. Plagiarism or literary fraud are certainly not correct terms for this practice. It was commonly known and accepted. Thus, the author (or authors) of the two Letters to Timothy and the one to Titus wrote what Paul *would* have said and in any case *should* have said, even though some of the content is quite at odds with his spirit. 1 Peter is a piece of Pauline thinking and was probably assigned the other apostle's name to give it credibility in circles that would have had nothing to do with Paul. The Letter to the Hebrews became associated with St. Paul back when people thought he should have written fourteen letters (two sevenses). But from early times, the learned knew Hebrews could not have been his work.

11. *How the Bible Came to Be.* The Books of the First Testament were in a fluid state, undergoing constant revisions and additions, until some time around Jesus' day. The rabbis then called a halt and provided a fixed text with all its duplications and occasional textually corrupt readings. The Second Testament books did not have as many adventures because they were not nearly so long in the process of composition. We know a little about the shape of the Gospels before their present shape, but not much. The two Letters of Paul to the Corinthians are edited versions of five or six different Letters. Philippians, too, short as it is, seems to be a compilation. When a book is the work of two or more writers—as Isaiah, Zechariah, and the five Books of Moses (among others) clearly are— one can ask whom the Holy Spirit inspired to bring them into existence. One answer is "the final editor of the book as we have it," but there are other, equally plausible answers. The Church says simply of the books in its canon of seventy-two, "All are inspired in all their parts." It was late in the fourth century when Christians began to list all these books as making up their Scriptures. There has never been a Church definition of how inspiration works or which of the many writers concerned were the subject of it.

12. *The One Thing Necessary.* The important matter about every part of the Bible is what it teaches about God and about humans' relations to God. It is a book about right conduct but chiefly religious conduct—namely, how God is to be praised, thanked, petitioned, and responded to as God speaks to Israel, the Church, the peoples of the world, and the people around us. God is just as central to the Second Testament as to the First. Jesus taught about the God of Israel whom he called "my Father," encouraging others to call him "our Father." When the early disciples proclaimed Jesus Christ crucified and risen, he was always presented as the way to God. The importance Jesus has for us is his grasp of the greatness and the intimate presence to us of God whose only Son he is in the power of the Spirit.

13. *Israel and Christians as Learners.* We need to look for a development of the religious ideas within the First Testament. There is probably development within the Second Testament, too, but it is harder to identify. Because the time of composition is brief—perhaps only fifty years—development is not easy to determine within it. Early in the Bible, the Israelites worshiped their God and assumed their neighbors worshiped theirs. Much later, perhaps after their sixth-century return from Babylonian exile, they began to think there was only one God over all, the one they called YHVH. Similarly, believers in Jesus show themselves slow in the New Testament books to learn his teaching of universal love and forgiveness.

14. *More Progress in Learning.* Early in the biblical period, the assumption was that if Israel served God faithfully, not only individuals but the whole people would be rewarded in this life. When death came to a person short of fullness of years or Israel was defeated in war, it was taken to be a divine punishment. Later, the Book of Jeremiah taught that the sins of the fathers did not bring punishment on the sons. Everyone was responsible for his own wrongdoing. Later still, the authors of Qoheleth and Job broke an age-old pattern by teaching that there was no relation between suffering or misfortune and wrongdoing. The just were as liable to suffer as the wicked.

All anyone could do was honor God and marvel at the mysterious divine will. Moreover, there is no clear belief in an afterlife for most of the biblical period. At most, there was a shadowy existence in the vicinity of the grave. With the Maccabean uprising (167–65 B.C.) there developed a belief in the resurrection of the dead at the Last Day. Both the Pharisees and Jesus and his associates were committed to this belief. The aristocratic Sadducees were not, chiefly because they recognized only the five Books of Moses in which a life to come is not mentioned.

14. *Inspiration's Power and Its Limits.* The Bible is a collection of books written by people for people of their own time. The authors had all the limitations of knowledge and outlook we might expect of people of their cultures—at first tribal and primitive, later advanced agricultural and urban—in Jesus' day, much influenced by the Greek language and philosophy. The gift of divine inspiration widened their religious horizons but did nothing to educate them about other matters. Consequently, we should not expect the biblical authors to know any more about the formation of the universe or animal and plant biology than ordinary observation could tell them. The Bible is free of error in all the religious truth by which its people needed to live. In an earlier Christian period, it was thought "inerrant" in all matters, but believers had to stop thinking that with the explosion of human knowledge that began in the West some 400 years ago. The doctrine of a totally error-free Bible was resurrected in the last century by Christians fearful of the threat posed by Darwin's discoveries and the scientism that followed. Holding fast to total biblical inerrance can lead to some fairly absurd positions. A good principle of interpretation emerged from the Galileo controversy: "God gave us the Bible to tell us how to go to heaven, not how the heavens go."

15. *Avoiding Being Shocked by the Bible.* The characters in both Testaments let us know how noble and just people can be when they let God guide their actions, and how low they can fall when they rely on their own cleverness and strength.

We modern Bible readers should not feel superior to the Israelites over the cruel way they waged war and kept slaves. We sink to far lower depths in the conduct of our own wars and let people live in dire poverty to keep our living standards high. Bemoaning biblical morality is time that would be better spent in using the Bible as a mirror of contemporary crimes and follies.

16. *The Prophets' True Function.* The books of the Prophets contain a message about public morality and politics in their day. These authors wrote about the immediate future of their times. They said that the evil actions of the rich and powerful, including men of religion, would shortly have visible consequences. They had no message for the far-distant future except this one: God would ultimately vindicate Israel. The Apocalypse (Revelation) of John is chiefly about the obscene wealth of the Roman Empire which God would in time bring low. The only message it has for the twentieth (or the fortieth) century is that the accumulation of wealth and power will bring in its train violence against the innocent whom God will vindicate in a way unknown to us. It does not reveal specific events of later ages.

17. *Prophecy and Fulfillment about Jesus.* The way to read the prophecies about Jesus is the way they were written, namely backwards. Believers in Jesus as the risen Christ combed the Bible and found him spoken of there because they already believed in him. Reading the Gospels and the other New Testament books carefully will show this. Jews and Gentiles who did not believe in him did not find him prophesied there. Previous faith in him would be necessary to do so. St. Augustine got this straight after four centuries of Christians' charging Jews with the impossible. "Do not say to a person," Augustine wrote, " 'Understand [these Scriptures] that you may believe.' Say, rather, 'Believe, so that you may understand [them].' " When the New Testament authors find in Jesus the person spoken of by all the prophets, it is because they first believe him to be such. Every line of the Hebrew Scriptures then confirms their previous conviction.

18. *Jewish "Blindness" a Nonstarter.* The New Testament writers could not comprehend why Jews in large numbers did not heed their preaching. The fact was that by far the greater number of Jews in their day never heard it. These inspired authors must be viewed sympathetically in their anger. They should not be credited fully when they charge their Jewish contemporaries with "resistance to the gospel." The use of "scribes and Pharisees" in Matthew, Mark, and Luke is probably in good part code language for some of the evangelists' contemporaries. The exact exchanges in which Jesus engaged over Law observance are all but impossible to reconstruct. St. John's "Jews" are no doubt the Judean power class of Jesus' day, but even more likely, they are the adversaries of the believers in Jesus who are contemporary with John. They may even have included ethnic Jews who believed in Jesus but in a wrong way according to John's standard. The bitter polemical writing of the first century should tell us *nothing* about how subsequent Christian relations with Jews should be carried on.

19. *Getting the Most out of St. Paul.* The Epistles of Paul have much to say to us about how to live "in Christ." His developed argument, in Galatians and Romans especially, requires a lot of background if we are to comprehend it. Even then, there is much in these letters that we cannot put to use. The rabbinic techniques he employs are too complex. There are two notable exceptions that we *can* understand: salvation will come to us by grace through faith, a truism which for Paul never absolves anyone from human effort; and God will never, can never, abandon the people of special divine favor, the Jews.

20. *Discovering the Kind of Writing before Us.* Everything the Bible says is of potential spiritual profit. For this to be true, we need to know with what kind of writing we are faced. Is a book or a passage figurative or literal? In other words, how does the author wish to be understood? We may have before us a piece of ancient legislation that no Jew or Christian comprehends, let alone keeps as it stands. Is this biblical book a play, an edifying tale, a spoof (as much of Jonah is), a collection of maxims (as Proverbs and James are in their different ways)?

What does the incredible longevity of the pre-Abraham people mean to express? How seriously can the male-dominated culture of both testaments be taken by us Christians of the West who are fully committed to the equality of the sexes? Why does not the Bible have anything to say about contraception, abortion, wife battering, child abuse, or organ transplants? In brief, for whom was it written and why?

Such riches there are, lying before us! (Have you made plans to start your Bible study group yet?)